GRATEFULNESS

I am **GEORGE SARANGO**, graduate in business sciences and white of books like one **GRATEFULNESS**.

My thanks to my family, my 4 daughters Silvana, Eveling , Lorens and Bea.

INDEX

GRATEFULNESS

INTRODUCTION

In the hustle and bustle of our daily lives, amidst the challenges we face and the goals we strive to achieve, there exists a timeless and profound practice that has the power to transform our homes, our relationships, and our lives: gratefulness.

Gratitude, the art of recognizing and appreciating the beauty and blessings that surround us, is a universal language that knows no boundaries.

It is a sentiment that transcends cultures, religions, and backgrounds, and it has the extraordinary ability to unite us as families in a shared sense of appreciation and love.

This book is an invitation to embark on a journey of discovery—a journey that will take you within the walls of your own home, where the seeds of gratitude can be sown and nurtured, where the echoes of appreciation can reverberate through the corridors of your heart and the hearts of your loved ones.

It's an exploration of how you can create a household filled with gratitude, where thankfulness becomes a way of life and where every day is an opportunity to acknowledge the abundance that surrounds you.

The family unit, as the cornerstone of society, is the ideal place to cultivate the practice of gratefulness.

Within your family, you have the power to shape the attitudes, values, and emotional landscapes of the next generation.

By weaving the threads of gratitude into the fabric of your family life, you can impart not only a deep sense of appreciation for life's blessings but also the resilience and strength that come from focusing on the positive.

In the chapters that follow, you will find a wealth of ideas, practices, and insights to help you infuse your family's everyday life with gratitude.

We will explore the power of shared gratitude rituals, the joy of expressing appreciation for one another, and the transformative effects of living with an open heart.

You will discover how gratitude can mend relationships, soothe the rough edges of adversity, and foster a deep sense of belonging within your family circle.

From gratitude journals to family meetings, from random acts of kindness to the simple act of saying "thank you," you will find a diverse array of tools and practices to tailor to your family's unique needs and dynamics.

As you navigate this journey, you'll not only uncover the many ways in which gratitude can bring you closer together but also how it can ripple outward, impacting your community and the world at large.

The stories within these pages are stories of everyday people like you and me—families who have chosen to embrace gratitude and have witnessed its remarkable transformations.

Their experiences serve as beacons of hope and inspiration, illuminating the path toward a more harmonious, loving, and grateful family life.

So, join us as we embark on this extraordinary voyage—a voyage that will lead you back to the heart of your family, where you will uncover the timeless wisdom of gratefulness and create a home filled with warmth, appreciation, and boundless love.

It is our hope that, through this journey, you will discover the immense potential for growth, healing, and joy that lies within the practice of gratefulness.

Together, let us unlock the transformative power of gratitude within your family home.

CHAPTER 1 THE POWER OF GRATITUDE

Setting the stage for the book by explaining the significance of gratitude in our lives.

Defining Gratitude

Providing a clear definition of gratitude and its different forms, such as appreciation, thankfulness, and recognition.

The Historical Perspective

Exploring the historical roots of gratitude, including its role in various cultures, religions, and philosophies.

The Science Behind Gratitude

Discussing the psychological and physiological effects of gratitude on individuals, including improved mental health, reduced stress, and increased overall well-being.

Gratitude vs. Ingratitude

Highlighting the contrast between a grateful mindset and one characterized by ingratitude, and the impact each can have on our lives.

The Gratitude Loop

Explaining the concept of the "gratitude loop," where practicing gratitude leads to more positive experiences, reinforcing the habit.

Gratitude and Resilience

Examining how gratitude can enhance our ability to bounce back from adversity and overcome challenges.

Cultivating Gratitude

Offering practical tips and strategies for cultivating gratitude in everyday life, including keeping a gratitude journal, mindfulness exercises, and expressing thanks to others.

Sharing real-life stories and examples of individuals who have experienced transformative changes in their lives through the practice of gratitude.

Gratitude's Role in Society

Discussing how gratitude can promote social cohesion and improve relationships within communities and organizations.

Gratitude and Personal Growth

Exploring how a grateful attitude can contribute to personal growth, self-improvement, and a greater sense of purpose.

Summarizing the key takeaways from the chapter and emphasizing the importance of recognizing the power of gratitude as a fundamental aspect of human existence.

This expanded outline for Chapter 1 provides a more detailed overview of the topics that could be covered in a book exploring the power and significance of gratitude in our lives.

CHAPTER 2 CULTIVATING A GRATEFUL HEART

Setting the stage for the chapter by highlighting the importance of actively cultivating gratitude in our lives.

Understanding the Grateful Heart

Defining what it means to have a "grateful heart" and how it differs from occasional feelings of thankfulness.

The Benefits of Cultivating Gratitude

Exploring the numerous psychological, emotional, and physical benefits of developing a grateful disposition.

Barriers to Gratitude

Identifying common obstacles that can hinder the cultivation of gratitude, such as negativity bias, entitlement, and a fast-paced lifestyle.

Mindfulness and Gratitude

Explaining how mindfulness practices can help individuals become more attuned to moments of gratitude in their daily lives.

Gratitude Journaling

Offering guidance on how to start and maintain a gratitude journal, including tips on what to write and how often to journal.

Daily Gratitude Practices

Providing a range of practical exercises and rituals that can help foster a grateful mindset, such as morning gratitude routines and gratitude meditation.

Gratitude Challenges

Introducing the concept of gratitude challenges, where individuals set specific goals to express gratitude more frequently.

The Role of Perspective

Discussing the importance of shifting one's perspective to find gratitude even in challenging or difficult situations.

Teaching Gratitude to Children

Exploring strategies for instilling gratitude in children and young adults, emphasizing its importance in their development.

Gratitude in Relationships

Examining how cultivating gratitude can enhance relationships, including romantic partnerships, friendships, and family connections.

Maintaining a Grateful Heart

Addressing the idea that cultivating gratitude is an ongoing practice, and providing advice on how to sustain a grateful mindset over time.

Sharing real-life stories of individuals who have successfully cultivated a grateful heart and the positive impact it has had on their lives.

Summarizing the key takeaways from the chapter and inspiring readers to embark on their own journey of cultivating a grateful heart.

This expanded outline for Chapter 2 delves into the various aspects of actively nurturing and developing a grateful heart, providing readers with both the understanding and practical tools they need to embrace gratitude as a way of life.

CHAPTER 3 GRATITUDE IN EVERY LIFE

Setting the stage for the chapter by emphasizing the practical importance of incorporating gratitude into daily routines.

The Grateful Morning Routine

Learning how starting the day with gratitude can set a positive tone, including practices such as morning gratitude reflections and affirmations.

Gratitude in the Workplace

Discussing the role of gratitude in the professional world, from fostering a positive work environment to improving job satisfaction.

Gratitude at Home

Highlighting the significance of expressing gratitude within the family unit, including the benefits of open communication and appreciation.

Gratitude in Parenting

Offering advice and strategies for parents on instilling gratitude in their children, creating a harmonious and appreciative home environment.

Gratitude in Friendship

Exploring how cultivating gratitude can deepen and strengthen friendships, with a focus on reciprocity and genuine appreciation.

Gratitude in Leisure Activities

Discussing how to incorporate gratitude into hobbies, interests, and recreational pursuits, enhancing the enjoyment of life's simple pleasures.

Practicing Gratitude on the Go

Offering tips for maintaining a grateful mindset even in busy, on-the-go situations, such as during commutes or errands.

The Role of Technology

Examining how technology can either hinder or facilitate gratitude and suggesting ways to use it mindfully in this context.

The Grateful Evening Routine

Estading the benefits of reflecting on gratitude at the end of the day, including practices like keeping a gratitude journal or sharing thankful moments with loved ones.

Gratitude in the Face of Adversity

Discussing how practicing gratitude during challenging times can foster resilience and provide a sense of hope and perspective.

Gratitude and Personal Finance

Addressing the connection between financial well-being and gratitude, emphasizing the importance of managing money with appreciation.

Cultural and Regional Perspectives

Recognizing that expressions of gratitude may vary across cultures and regions, highlighting the universal nature of gratitude despite these differences.

Case Studies

Sharing real-life examples of individuals who have integrated gratitude into their daily lives and the positive transformations they've experienced.

Summarizing the key takeaways from the chapter and inspiring readers to incorporate gratitude into their everyday lives, recognizing the potential for profound positive change.

This expanded outline for this Chapter provides a comprehensive look at how gratitude can be woven into the fabric of daily life, from morning routines to workplace interactions, family dynamics, and leisure activities, emphasizing its relevance and practicality in various aspects of life.

CHAPTER 4 THE SCIENCE OF GRATITUDE

Setting the stage for the chapter by emphasizing the importance of understanding the scientific basis of gratitude and its effects on our well-being.

Psychology of Gratitude

Exploring the psychological aspects of gratitude, including the role of positive emotions, mindfulness, and personal growth.

Neuroscience of Gratitude

Delving into the neurological processes associated with gratitude, such as the release of dopamine and oxytocin, and how they contribute to feelings of happiness and social bonding.

Positive Psychology and Gratitude

Discussing the field of positive psychology and its connection to gratitude, as well as the works of researchers like Martin Seligman and positive psychology interventions (PPIs).

Gratitude and Emotional Well-Being

Examining how practicing gratitude can improve emotional regulation, reduce symptoms of depression and anxiety, and enhance overall mental health.

Gratitude and Physical Health

Discussing the impact of gratitude on physical health, including its potential to reduce stress, boost the immune system, and promote better sleep.

Social Aspects of Gratitude

Exploring how gratitude strengthens social bonds, promotes prosocial

behavior, and contributes to the formation and maintenance of relationships.

Gratitude and Resilience

Discussing the role of gratitude in building resilience and helping individuals navigate adversity more effectively.

Cultural and Cross-Cultural Perspectives

Addressing how cultural and regional factors influence the experience and expression of gratitude, with a focus on the global applicability of gratitude research.

Research Findings and Studies

Summarizing key findings from scientific studies and experiments related to gratitude, showcasing the evidence-based benefits of gratitude practices.

Practical Applications

Offering practical advice on how individuals can leverage scientific insights to incorporate gratitude into their daily lives for maximum benefit.

The Intersection of Spirituality and Science

Discussing the relationship between gratitude, spirituality, and well-being, and how these elements converge in the scientific study of gratitude.

Gratitude Interventions

Exploring specific gratitude interventions and exercises that have been developed based on scientific research, along with instructions for implementing them.

Critiques and Controversies

Acknowledging any critiques or controversies within the field of gratitude research and providing a balanced perspective on the limitations of scientific studies.

Summarizing the key takeaways from the chapter and emphasizing the significance of understanding the science of gratitude in harnessing its potential for personal growth and well-being.

This expanded outline for Chapter 4 delves into the scientific underpinnings of gratitude, from psychology and neuroscience to the positive psychology movement, offering readers a deeper understanding of why and how gratitude practices can have such profound effects on their lives.

CHAPTER 5 GRATITUDE IN RELATIONSHIPS

Setting the stage for the chapter by highlighting the pivotal role of gratitude in fostering healthy and meaningful relationships.

The Importance of Gratitude in Relationships

Emphasizing the significance of expressing gratitude in various types of relationships, including romantic, familial, and friendships.

Gratitude and Romantic Relationships

Discussing how gratitude can enhance the quality of romantic partnerships, improve communication, and create a deeper emotional connection.

Gratitude in Parent-Child Relationships

Exploring the unique dynamics of gratitude in parent-child relationships, including its role in strengthening bonds and fostering positive development in children.

Gratitude Among Friends

Examining how gratitude can deepen friendships, increase trust, and create a supportive social network.

Gratitude in Workplace Relationships

Discussing the application of gratitude in professional settings, including its potential to improve teamwork, leadership, and employee satisfaction.

The Art of Giving and Receiving Gratitude

Exploring the reciprocal nature of gratitude in relationships and the benefits of both expressing and receiving appreciation.

Challenges in Expressing Gratitude

Addressing common obstacles that may hinder the expression of gratitude in relationships, such as pride, miscommunication, and emotional barriers.

Gratitude Rituals for Couples

Offering practical suggestions for couples to incorporate gratitude rituals into their daily routines or special occasions.

Teaching Children Gratitude in Relationships

Providing strategies for parents and caregivers to teach children the value of gratitude within their family and social relationships.

Maintaining Gratitude Through Relationship Challenges

Discussing how gratitude can act as a stabilizing force during conflicts or difficult periods in relationships.

Cultural and Gender Perspectives

Recognizing how cultural norms and gender dynamics may influence the expression and reception of gratitude in different types of relationships.

Sharing real-life stories and experiences of individuals and couples who have transformed their relationships through the practice of gratitude.

Long-Term Effects of Gratitude in Relationships

Examining the sustained benefits of incorporating gratitude into relationships, including increased satisfaction and resilience over time.

Summarizing the key takeaways from the chapter and inspiring readers to apply the principles of gratitude to nurture and strengthen their relationships.

This expanded outline for this Chapter provides a comprehensive exploration of how gratitude can be a powerful catalyst for building and maintaining positive, meaningful connections with others in various facets of life.

CHAPTER 6 OVERCOMING CHALLENGES WITH GRATITUDE

Setting the stage for the chapter by highlighting the transformative role of gratitude in navigating and surmounting life's challenges.

The Resilience of Gratitude

Discussing how gratitude serves as a powerful tool for building resilience in the face of adversity, such as illness, loss, or difficult life transitions.

Gratitude and Coping Strategies

Exploring how gratitude practices can complement various coping strategies, including problem-solving, emotional regulation, and seeking social support.

Finding Gratitude in Loss

Sharing stories and examples of individuals who have used gratitude to cope with the loss of loved ones, emphasizing the healing power of acknowledging the positive memories and impacts of those who have passed.

Health Challenges and Gratitude

Discussing how gratitude can play a role in managing chronic illnesses, improving mental health outcomes, and enhancing the overall well-being of individuals facing health challenges.

Gratitude and Financial Hardships

Examining how gratitude can help individuals reframe their perspective on financial difficulties, reduce stress related to money, and foster a sense of abundance even in times of scarcity.

Gratitude in the Face of Trauma

Discussing the use of gratitude as a coping mechanism for individuals who have experienced trauma, emphasizing the importance of professional support alongside gratitude practices.

Gratitude as a Tool for Post-Traumatic Growth

Exploring how gratitude can contribute to post-traumatic growth, allowing individuals to find meaning, resilience, and positive change following trauma.

The Role of Supportive Relationships

Emphasizing how the expression and reception of gratitude within supportive relationships can be especially crucial during challenging times.

Gratitude and Stress Reduction

Discussing the physiological and psychological benefits of gratitude in reducing stress, managing anxiety, and improving overall mental well-being.

The Connection Between Gratitude and Problem-Solving

Examining how a grateful mindset can enhance problem-solving skills, creativity, and adaptability in the face of challenges.

Cultural and Cross-Cultural Perspectives on Resilience

Recognizing cultural and regional differences in how gratitude is applied as a tool for resilience and coping.

Sharing real-life stories of individuals who have overcome significant challenges by integrating gratitude into their coping strategies.

Sustaining Gratitude Through Ongoing Challenges

Discussing how to maintain gratitude practices over the long term, even when faced with ongoing difficulties or adversity.

Summarizing the key takeaways from the chapter and inspiring readers to harness the power of gratitude as a means of resilience and growth in the face of life's challenges.

This expanded outline for this Chapter provides a comprehensive exploration of how gratitude can be a source of strength, resilience, and hope when confronting adversity and life's most significant challenges.

CHAPTER 7 EXPRESSING THANKS AND APPRECIATION

Setting the stage for the chapter by emphasizing the importance of actively expressing gratitude and appreciation in our lives.

Why Expressing Gratitude Matters

Discussing the benefits of outwardly expressing thanks and appreciation, both for the giver and the recipient.

The Different Forms of Expressing Gratitude

Exploring the various ways people can express gratitude, including verbal expressions, written notes, gestures, and acts of kindness.

The Art of Saying "Thank You"

Offering guidance on how to effectively and genuinely say "thank you," including tips on tone, timing, and sincerity.

The Power of Handwritten Notes

Discussing the impact of handwritten letters and notes in a digital age, and providing tips for crafting heartfelt messages of gratitude.

The Role of Non-Verbal Communication

Exploring the significance of non-verbal expressions of gratitude, such as body language, facial expressions, and gestures.

Expressing Gratitude in the Workplace

Discussing the importance of recognition and appreciation in professional settings, including strategies for managers and leaders to acknowledge their team's efforts.

Family Traditions of Gratitude

Sharing examples of family traditions and rituals that revolve around expressing thanks and appreciation, promoting a culture of gratitude within the home.

Gratitude and Acts of Kindness

Discussing the connection between gratitude and performing acts of kindness, highlighting how small gestures can make a significant impact.

Teaching Children to Express Gratitude

Providing strategies for parents and educators to teach children how to express thanks and appreciation in age-appropriate ways.

Gratitude and Generosity

Exploring the link between gratitude and generosity, with a focus on how expressing gratitude can lead to a desire to give back.

Cultural and Cross-Cultural Perspectives on Expressing Gratitude

Recognizing cultural norms and regional differences in how gratitude is expressed and the etiquette associated with expressing thanks.

Overcoming Barriers to Expressing Gratitude

Addressing common obstacles that may hinder individuals from expressing gratitude and providing strategies to overcome them.

Expressing Gratitude Through Creative Outlets

Discussing how art, music, and other creative forms can be used to convey gratitude and appreciation.

Sharing real-life stories of individuals and organizations that have transformed their relationships and environments through the regular expression of gratitude.

Summarizing the key takeaways from the chapter and inspiring readers to actively incorporate expressions of thanks and appreciation into their daily lives.

This expanded outline for these pages offers a comprehensive exploration of the various ways in which people can express gratitude and appreciation, encouraging readers to harness the positive impact of these expressions in their relationships and interactions with others.

CHAPTER 8   GRATITUDE AND WELL-BEING

Setting the stage for the chapter by emphasizing the profound connection between gratitude and overall well-being.

Defining Well-Being

Exploring the multifaceted nature of well-being, including its physical, emotional, social, and psychological dimensions.

Gratitude as a Pillar of Well-Being

Discussing how gratitude can be considered a foundational element of well-being, contributing to greater life satisfaction and fulfillment.

Positive Psychology and Well-Being

Introducing the principles of positive psychology and its emphasis on strengths, virtues, and flourishing, with a focus on gratitude as a central component.

The Impact of Gratitude on Happiness

Examining the direct relationship between gratitude and happiness, as well as the ways in which gratitude can enhance positive emotions.

Gratitude and Stress Reduction

Discussing how practicing gratitude can mitigate stress, lower cortisol levels, and promote relaxation and emotional resilience.

Enhancing Emotional Resilience

Exploring how gratitude can help individuals bounce back from setbacks, cope with challenges, and maintain emotional balance.

Gratitude and Physical Health

Discussing the connection between gratitude and physical well-being, including its potential to boost the immune system, lower blood pressure, and promote better sleep.

Gratitude and Relationships

Highlighting how gratitude contributes to healthier and more satisfying relationships, thereby enhancing social and emotional well-being.

The Role of Gratitude in Self-Improvement

Examining how gratitude can motivate individuals to engage in personal growth, self-reflection, and goal achievement.

Gratitude and Life Satisfaction

Discussing the link between gratitude and overall life satisfaction, emphasizing the importance of appreciating the present moment.

The Flow of Positive Psychology Interventions (PPIs)

Exploring the various positive psychology interventions related to gratitude and their effects on overall well-being.

Cultural and Cross-Cultural Perspectives on Well-Being

Recognizing how cultural values and norms can influence perceptions of well-being and the expression of gratitude.

Barriers to Integrating Gratitude and Well-Being

Addressing common challenges and misconceptions that may hinder individuals from incorporating gratitude into their pursuit of well-being.

Gratitude as a Lifelong Practice

Discussing the idea that gratitude is a lifelong journey and how individuals can continually deepen their sense of well-being through gratitude practices.

Sharing real-life stories of individuals who have experienced remarkable transformations in their overall well-being through the regular practice of gratitude.

Summarizing the key takeaways from the chapter and inspiring readers to recognize the profound impact of gratitude on their well-being and overall quality of life.

This expanded outline for this pages provides a comprehensive examination of how gratitude is intricately linked to various dimensions of well-being, encouraging readers to embrace gratitude as a powerful tool for living a more fulfilling and balanced life.

CHAPTER 9 GRATITUDE PRACTICES AND RITUALS

Setting the stage for the chapter by emphasizing the practical application of gratitude through structured practices and rituals.

The Role of Consistency

Discussing the importance of regular gratitude practices in cultivating a grateful mindset and reaping the associated benefits.

Gratitude Journaling

Exploring the practice of keeping a gratitude journal, including tips on how to get started, what to write, and the benefits of this daily ritual.

Mindfulness and Gratitude

Discussing how mindfulness practices can be integrated with gratitude, such as mindful gratitude meditation and reflection.

Gratitude Meditation

Providing guidance on mindfulness meditation techniques focused on gratitude, helping individuals develop a deeper sense of appreciation.

The Gratitude Letter

Exploring the practice of writing gratitude letters to express appreciation to individuals who have positively impacted one's life.

Gratitude Affirmations

Discussing the use of gratitude affirmations and mantras to reframe thoughts and foster a more positive outlook.

Gratitude Rituals for Couples and Families

Offering suggestions for couples and families to incorporate gratitude practices into their routines, enhancing their relationships.

Gratitude Walks and Nature Connection

Exploring the practice of taking gratitude walks in natural settings to foster a deeper connection with the environment.

Random Acts of Kindness

Discussing the concept of performing random acts of kindness as a way of expressing gratitude and spreading positivity.

Gratitude Challenges

Introducing structured gratitude challenges and initiatives that encourage individuals to express thanks and appreciation consistently.

Digital Gratitude Practices

Discussing the role of technology in supporting gratitude practices, including gratitude apps and online communities.

Customizing Gratitude Practices

Encouraging readers to tailor gratitude practices to their personal preferences and needs, emphasizing flexibility and creativity.

Overcoming Common Challenges

Addressing potential obstacles individuals may encounter when trying to establish and maintain gratitude practices, and offering solutions.

Cultural and Cross-Cultural Perspectives on Gratitude Practices

Recognizing how cultural and regional influences can shape the types of gratitude practices and rituals embraced by individuals.

Long-Term Commitment to Gratitude

Emphasizing the idea that gratitude practices should become long-term commitments and part of an ongoing journey toward personal growth.

Sharing real-life examples of individuals and communities that have experienced positive transformations through the consistent practice of gratitude.

Summarizing the key takeaways from the chapter and inspiring readers to incorporate gratitude practices and rituals into their daily lives for lasting change.

This expanded outline for Chapter 9 provides a comprehensive exploration of various gratitude practices and rituals, offering readers a range of options to choose from based on their preferences and lifestyles while highlighting the importance of consistency and personalization in cultivating gratitude.

CHAPTER 10 THE TRANSFORMATIVE NATURE OF GRATITUDE

Setting the stage for the chapter by emphasizing the profound and transformative impact that gratitude can have on one's life.

The Power of Shifted Perspectives

Discussing how gratitude can transform one's perspective, enabling them to see opportunities, beauty, and positivity even in challenging circumstances.

Gratitude as a Catalyst for Change

Exploring how a grateful mindset can serve as a catalyst for personal growth, self-improvement, and positive life changes.

Transforming Negative Emotions

Discussing how gratitude can be used to transform negative emotions, such as anger, envy, or resentment, into more positive and constructive feelings.

Gratitude and Forgiveness

Examining the role of gratitude in the process of forgiveness, emphasizing how it can facilitate healing and reconciliation.

Gratitude and Self-Compassion

Exploring the connection between self-compassion and gratitude, highlighting how self-appreciation can lead to self-improvement.

Overcoming Entitlement

Discussing how practicing gratitude can help individuals overcome feelings of entitlement and develop a more appreciative and humble attitude.

Gratitude and Personal Relationships

Highlighting how gratitude can transform relationships, fostering deeper connections, trust, and appreciation among individuals.

Gratitude and Life Goals

Exploring how gratitude can help individuals set and achieve meaningful life goals, guiding them toward a more purposeful and fulfilling future.

Gratitude and Generosity

Discussing the link between gratitude and generosity, emphasizing how gratitude can inspire individuals to give back to their communities and society.

Gratitude and Resilience

Examining how gratitude enhances resilience, helping individuals bounce back from setbacks and develop a stronger capacity to handle adversity.

The Journey of Self-Discovery

Discussing how practicing gratitude can lead to a deeper understanding of oneself, uncovering values, strengths, and passions.

Cultural and Cross-Cultural Perspectives on Transformation

Recognizing the diversity of ways gratitude can lead to transformation, influenced by cultural values, traditions, and practices.

The Ripple Effect of Gratitude

Exploring how the transformative nature of gratitude can have a ripple effect, positively impacting not only individuals but also their communities and beyond.

Sharing real-life stories of individuals who have experienced profound personal transformation through the practice of gratitude.

Summarizing the key takeaways from the chapter and inspiring readers to recognize the potential for personal and societal transformation through gratitude.

This expanded outline for this book delves into the deep and transformative nature of gratitude, illustrating how it has the power to shift perspectives, inspire change, and create a ripple effect of positivity in both individual lives and the world at large.

CONCLUSIÓN

Concluding and reflecting on the Journey

Encourage readers to take a moment to reflect on their journey through the book and the insights they've gained about gratitude.

The Universal Power of Gratitude

Reiterate the universal nature of gratitude, emphasizing that it transcends cultural, religious, and personal boundaries.

Gratitude as a Way of Life

Emphasize that gratitude is not just an occasional practice but a way of life, and that its benefits are most fully realized through consistent effort.

Recognizing the Everyday Miracles

Remind readers of the beauty in everyday life and the power of gratitude in helping us recognize and appreciate these ordinary yet extraordinary moments.

The Ripple Effect of Gratitude

Highlight how the practice of gratitude has the potential to create a ripple effect, positively impacting not only our own lives but also those around us.

Inspiration from Real-Life Stories

Share some memorable stories and examples from the book of individuals and communities whose lives have been transformed by gratitude.

The Call to Action

Encourage readers to take action and incorporate gratitude into their lives, whether through simple daily practices or more elaborate rituals.

Sustaining the Grateful Mindset

Offer guidance on sustaining a grateful mindset in the face of challenges and adversity, emphasizing that gratitude is a lifelong journey.

Expressing Gratitude to Others

Remind readers of the importance of expressing gratitude to the people who have made a difference in their lives.

The Impact on Well-Being

Summarize the scientific evidence supporting the positive effects of gratitude on mental, emotional, physical, and social well-being.

Building a Grateful Community

Encourage readers to share their newfound appreciation and knowledge of gratitude with their communities, fostering a culture of thankfulness.

Gratitude Beyond the Self

Discuss how gratitude can extend beyond individual well-being to contribute to a more compassionate, empathetic, and connected society.

A Grateful Future

Paint a vision of a future where gratitude is a central tenet of our lives, contributing to a more harmonious and fulfilling world.

Closing Thoughts

Offer final reflections on the transformative power of gratitude and the potential for readers to lead more joyful, purposeful, and meaningful lives through its practice.

Gratitude is the Gift

Conclude by reiterating that gratitude is a gift we can give to ourselves and to the world, and that by embracing it, we can experience a more fulfilling and contented life.

Acknowledgments

Thank the readers for embarking on this journey of exploration and growth, and acknowledge their commitment to living a life of gratitude.

Final Gratitude

End the conclusion with a final expression of gratitude to all those who have contributed to the book and to the readers for their time and attention.

This book you'll want to leave your readers with a sense of inspiration and motivation to embrace gratitude as a fundamental aspect of their lives, and to recognize the potential for personal growth, positive change, and the creation of a more thankful and harmonious world through this practice.

Family Gratitude Journal:

Start a shared gratitude journal where family members can write down things they are thankful for each day.

Encourage everyone to contribute, whether it's big or small things.

Gratitude Rituals:

 Incorporate gratitude rituals into your daily routine. For example, during meals, take a moment to express gratitude for the food, the company, or any other positive aspect of the day.

Thankful Conversations:

Engage in meaningful conversations about gratitude.

Ask each family member to share something they're grateful for or a memorable gratitude experience.

This can be done at the dinner table or during family meetings.

Appreciation Notes:

Leave surprise notes of appreciation for each other around the house. These notes can be as simple as expressing love and gratitude for one another.

Gratitude Board or Wall:

Create a gratitude board or wall where family members can post sticky notes with their expressions of gratitude.

This visual display can serve as a daily reminder of all the things you appreciate.

Random Acts of Kindness:

Encourage family members to perform random acts of kindness for each other and for others outside the family.

This reinforces the idea of giving and receiving gratitude.

Family Thank-You Jar: Keep a jar where family members can write thank-you notes to each other.

When someone does something special or helpful, place a note in the jar to acknowledge and appreciate their efforts.

Share Accomplishments:

Celebrate each other's achievements and milestones.

Share in the joy of accomplishments, big or small, and express gratitude for each person's unique contributions.

Volunteer Together:

 Engage in family volunteering activities. Working together to help others in need can deepen the sense of gratitude and compassion within the family.

Gratitude Scavenger Hunt:

Organize a family scavenger hunt with a twist by looking for things to be grateful for in your home or neighborhood.

This encourages everyone to see their surroundings in a new light.

Family Meetings:

Hold regular family meetings to discuss goals and plans.

During these meetings, express gratitude for each other's support and collaboration.

Read Books on Gratitude:

Choose books or stories about gratitude to read together as a family.

Discuss the lessons learned and how they can be applied in your own lives.

Gratitude Crafts:

Create crafts or art projects that revolve around gratitude.

This can be a fun and creative way for family members to express their thankfulness.

Celebrate Gratitude Days:

Designate certain days or occasions as "Gratitude Days" where you spend extra time expressing appreciation for each other and reflecting on the things you're thankful for.

Lead by Example:

As parents or guardians, lead by example.

Show your own gratitude openly and consistently to inspire your children to do the same.

Cultivating gratitude is an ongoing process.

 By incorporating these practices into your family life, you can create a loving and appreciative atmosphere that benefits everyone and strengthens your bonds.

www.ingramcontent.com/pod-product-compliance
Lightning Source LLC
Chambersburg PA
CBHW050742260726
48661CB00001B/364